STEM Projects in **MINECRAFT**™

The Unofficial Guide to Growing Plants in MINECRAFT™

ERIC J. TOWER

PowerKiDS press

New York

Published in 2019 by The Rosen Publishing Group, Inc.
29 East 21st Street, New York, NY 10010

First Edition

Editor: Greg Roza
Book Design: Rachel Rising
Illustrator: Matías Lapegüe

Photo Credits: Cover, pp. 1, 3, 4, 6, 8, 10, 12, 14, 16, 18, 20, 22, 23, 24 (background) Evgeniy Dzyuba/Shutterstock.com; pp. 4, 6, 10, 14, 16, 20 (insert) Levent Konuk/Shutterstock.com; p. 7 Henning van Wyk/Shutterstock.com; p. 8 Salparadis/Shutterstock.com; p. 11 (insert) Ascent/PKS Media Inc./Getty Images; p. 18 Anton Foltin/Shutterstock.com; p. 22 Samuel Borges Photography/Shutterstock.com.

Library of Congress Cataloging-in-Publication Data

Names: Tower, Eric J., author.
Title: The unofficial guide to growing plants in Minecraft / Eric J. Tower.
Description: New York : PowerKids Press, [2019] | Series: STEM projects in
    Minecraft | Includes index.
Identifiers: LCCN 2018028608| ISBN 9781538342466 (library bound) | ISBN
    9781538342442 (paperback) | ISBN 9781538342459 (6 pack)
Subjects: LCSH: Growth (Plants)–Juvenile literature. | Minecraft
    (Game)–Juvenile literature.
Classification: LCC QK731 .T69 2019 | DDC 581.3–dc23
LC record available at https://lccn.loc.gov/2018028608

Manufactured in the United States of America

CPSIA Compliance Information: Batch #CWPK19. For Further Information contact Rosen Publishing, New York, New York at 1-800-237-9932

Contents

Let's Get Growing!

The world of *Minecraft* is filled with many useful plants. They can be harvested for food and to get wood for building. Just like in the real world, different types of plants need different amounts of water, light, heat, and soil to grow. Areas with these conditions of water, light, heat, and soil are called **biomes**. We'll talk about how best to grow important plants from every biome and what these plants are used for in *Minecraft* and in our world.

Minecraft is a sandbox game that takes place in a world made mostly of cubes. Let's get growing!

MINECRAFT MANIA

Minecraft can be played in several different **modes**. It is easiest to play in Creative mode. In this mode, you can use an unlimited number of plants and seeds that you would otherwise have to collect yourself. For an adventure, go back and try to find the seeds in the wild!

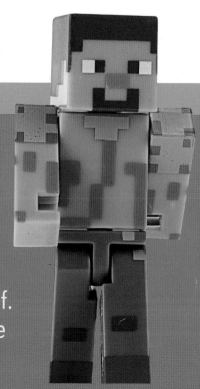

There are many biomes on Earth and in *Minecraft*, including desert, forest, and grassland biomes. Can you tell which plants grow in which biomes?

5

Seeds to Sow

Growing wheat in *Minecraft* works a lot like it did for early farmers over 10,000 years ago. Starting with wild plants, farmers collected seeds to **sow** in the ground. In *Minecraft*, you can collect seeds to grow wheat by hitting the tall grass that can be found in almost every biome. These seeds can be planted in any soil that has been tilled with a hoe.

The best place to grow wheat is a spot that gets a lot of sunlight. Soil that is within four blocks of water is considered **irrigated** and will grow plants much faster.

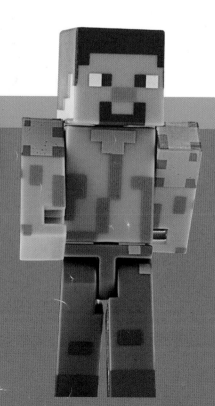

MINECRAFT MANIA

You can also grow potatoes, carrots, and beetroots in *Minecraft*. To grow potatoes or carrots, you plant one of the vegetables in tilled ground. To grow beetroots, you plant beetroot seeds.

5 BLOCKS
OF WATER

Minecraft wheat has eight stages of growth before it is ready to harvest. Just like in real life, you can use **bone meal** to **fertilize** the soil and speed up growth.

bone meal

7

Saplings

There are more than 60,000 types of trees in the real world. **Foresters** may tend to a forest the same way farmers tend to a field of wheat. They make sure seeds are planted in the right soil. Sometimes, they harvest the trees for wood.

In *Minecraft*, there are only six types of trees: oak, dark oak, spruce, acacia, jungle, and birch. Getting each type of tree to grow requires special attention when planting **saplings**. Different types of sapling need different amounts of space to grow. Oak trees require the least amount of space. Jungle trees and dark oak trees can require the most.

Each type of tree has different wood that you can use to
make boards to build boats, houses, and tools in *Minecraft*.

SPRUCE

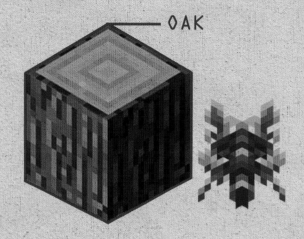

OAK

BIRCH

DARK OAK

ACACIA

JUNGLE

Tending the Forest

Tending to forests can be a hard job. Foresters make sure the trees are safe from fire, insects, and illnesses that could harm them. Sometimes they cut down older trees to make room for new trees to grow.

If you tend to a forest in *Minecraft*, be careful that your saplings have room to grow upward. A sapling will grow in almost any type of soil, but some trees may not grow if the ground around them is not level. Sometimes, you can use bone meal to get saplings to grow faster. A light source such as torches can be used to grow trees inside.

MINECRAFT MANIA

If you plant dark oak, spruce, or jungle tree saplings in a two-by-two square arrangement with enough space above them, they'll grow into giant trees. These trees only grow naturally in certain biomes, such as mega **taiga** biomes and jungle biomes. Dark oak saplings will only grow when planted together like this.

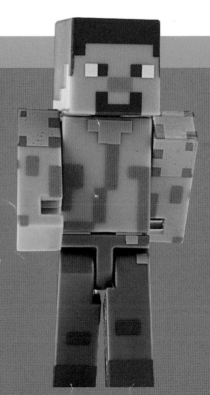

This forester is checking on the health of a spruce sapling in the forest.

SPRUCE TREE

Harvesting Trees

In the real world, lumberjacks harvest trees when they've grown. Foresters mark the trees with the most useful wood, and lumberjacks cut them down. Cut **timber** is sent to a lumber mill to be turned into boards. Foresters and lumberjacks work hard to make use of every part of a tree.

In *Minecraft*, you can also make use of the whole tree when you cut it down. Use your axe to collect not just the wood blocks to make boards but also to clear the leaf blocks. Leaf blocks may drop useful items such as apples or saplings that you can use to plant more trees in the future. You can also collect leaf blocks using shears, or clippers.

You can build with *Minecraft* wood with the bark still on or turn the wood into planks, or boards. Here's what the different woods and planks look like.

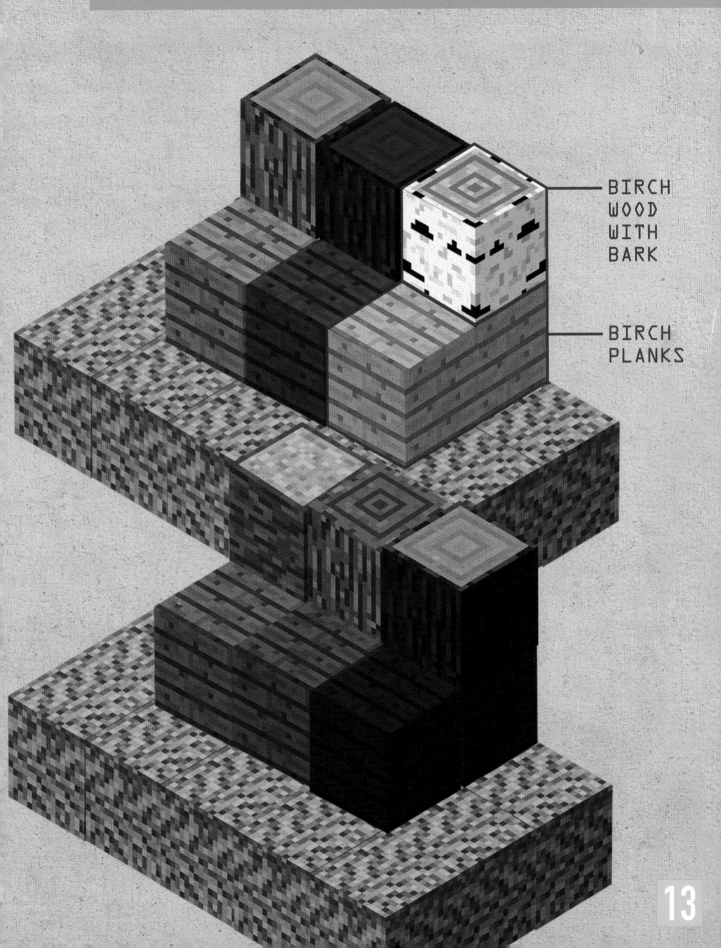

BIRCH
WOOD
WITH
BARK

BIRCH
PLANKS

13

Pumpkins and Melons

In the real world, some crops require a lot more water than others to grow. Real pumpkins and watermelons are over 90 percent water and require a lot more space to grow a good crop.

To farm pumpkins and melons in *Minecraft*, you also need lots of space and irrigated land. You can find pumpkins in most biomes, but melons only grow in jungle biomes. You can get seeds from the harvested pumpkins and melons. Each pumpkin or melon plant will need two blocks to grow. Plant the seeds in two rows next to each other. Pumpkins and melons that grow will appear in the rows to the side.

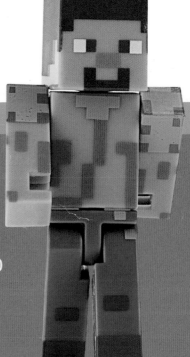

MINECRAFT MANIA

Sugar cane is another *Minecraft* crop. It grows wild in almost every soil type, but only next to water blocks. Plants can grow up to four blocks tall. Harvested sugar cane can be used to make sugar or create paper.

When it's time to harvest, take only the pumpkin or melon and leave the stem. The stem will continue to grow pumpkins and melons. Just like with other plants, you can speed up the growth with bone meal.

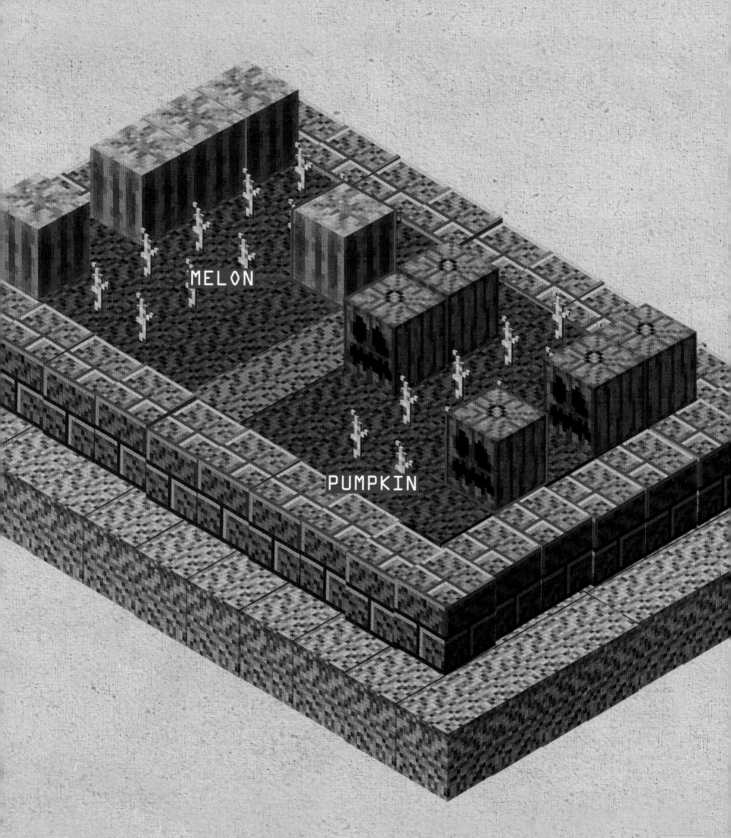

MELON

PUMPKIN

Growing Flowers

Floriculture is the science of flowering plants. There are over 400,000 flowering plants on Earth. Specialists called floriculturists grow flowers for use in many different ways. Flowers are used to make medicine, perfumes, and more. People use them for gifts for holidays such as Valentine's Day.

In *Minecraft*, there are 11 types of flowers: dandelions, poppies, blue orchids, alliums, azure bluets, tulips, oxeye daisies, sunflowers, lilacs, rose bushes, and peonies. *Minecraft* flowers don't have seeds. You can find flowers naturally or cause them to grow by applying bone meal to grassy areas. Each type of flower grows naturally in specific biomes, and the grassland biome grows the most kinds of flowers.

MINECRAFT MANIA

Just like in the real world, flowers are used in *Minecraft* to craft items. Dyes used to color wool and other things in *Minecraft* are made from flowers. Flowers can also be used to attract and breed wild rabbits.

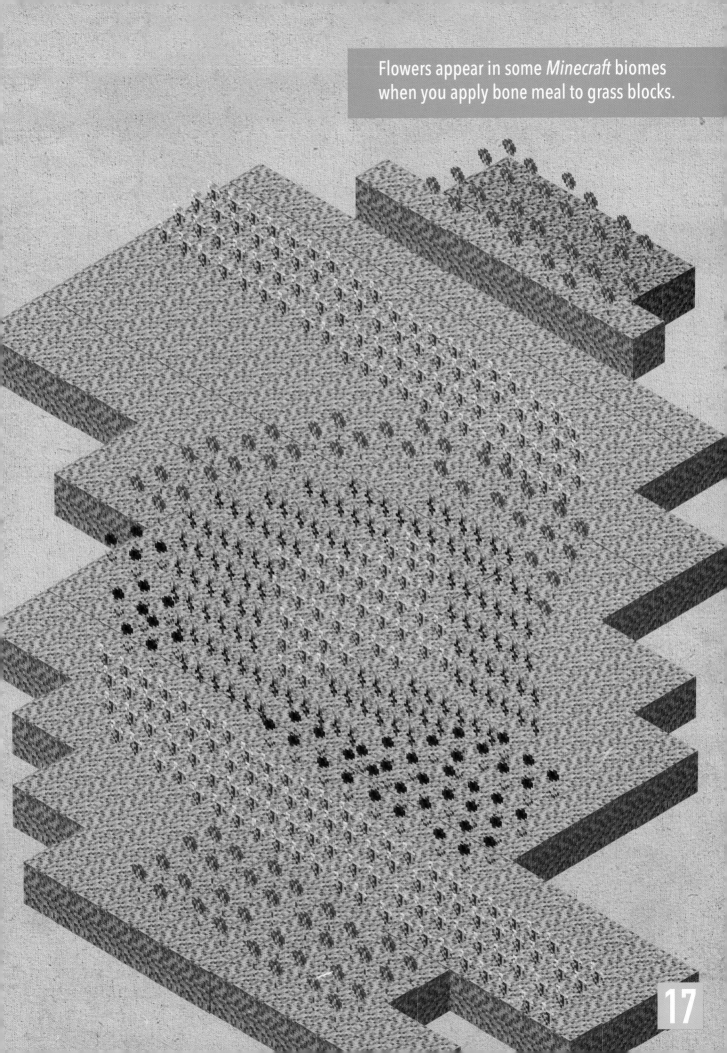

Flowers appear in some *Minecraft* biomes when you apply bone meal to grass blocks.

17

Hearty Cactus

Did you know that cacti are native to the Americas, but they're grown in many places for their fruit? There are more than 2,000 kinds of cacti. Most plants are hearty and require little water. This makes them perfect for desert biomes.

In *Minecraft*, there's only one type of cactus, and it only grows naturally in desert and **mesa** biomes. To plant a cactus, you need to harvest a cactus block from an existing cactus and place it on a sand block. Unlike in the real world, the *Minecraft* cactus doesn't need sunlight to grow. They can grow several blocks tall.

You can plant cacti almost anywhere in *Minecraft*, as long as there is sand under them. However, in the real world, they mostly grow naturally in dry places such as deserts.

Giant Mushrooms!

Mushrooms aren't really plants. They're **fungi**. There are nearly 100,000 kinds of fungi on Earth. Unlike plants, fungi don't require sunlight to grow and are often found in dark places. Mushrooms and other fungi are farmed for use as food and medicine.

In *Minecraft*, there are two basic types of mushrooms: red mushrooms and brown mushrooms. Small mushrooms can be found in dark places such as caves and in forests with lots of leaf cover. Some biomes have huge mushrooms the size of trees! You can apply bone meal to small mushrooms to grow them into big mushrooms.

MINECRAFT MANIA

Brewing is a form of crafting in *Minecraft*. With brewing, you can make potions that allow you to see in the dark, run faster, and jump farther. Mushrooms are used with other ingredients to make fermented spider eyes, an important potion item.

Mushrooms can be used to craft stews and as an ingredient in many **potions**, such as the Potion of Invisibility.

Making Mods

You can make your *Minecraft* creations even more exciting with modifications, or mods. Using a computer program called ScriptCraft, you can create new blocks, change the way the game functions, and make your own games. Imagine what you could create! You could create a farm for giants or a floating garden in the sky. You can even create villagers who will tend to your crops. You're only limited by your imagination!

If you're interested in learning how to create mods in *Minecraft*, visit the website below. You'll find the information needed to get started with ScriptCraft and build your own *Minecraft* mods.

https://scriptcraftjs.org/

Glossary

biome: A natural community of plants and animals, such as a forest or desert.

bone meal: A matter made from bones in *Minecraft* and the real world. It's used to fertilize land.

fertilize: To add a matter to soil to help plants grow.

forester: Someone who cares for a forest and trees.

fungus: A living thing that is like a plant but that doesn't have leaves, flowers, or green color or make its own food. The plural form is fungi.

irrigate: To supply water to land by man-made means.

mesa: A hill or mountain with steep sides and a level top. *Minecraft* mesas, however, have red sand and hills and towers made of many colors of clay.

mode: A form of something that is different from other forms of the same thing.

potion: A drink meant to have a special effect on someone.

sapling: A young tree.

sow: To plant seeds.

taiga: A forest near the Arctic region that has many evergreen trees.

timber: Wood used for building, or trees that are grown for their wood.

Index

B
beetroots, 6
biomes, 4, 5, 6, 10, 14,
    16, 17, 18, 20
bone meal, 7, 10, 15,
    16, 17, 20

C
cactus, 18, 19
carrots, 6
Creative mode, 4

D
dyes, 16

F
flowers, 16, 17
fungi, 20

H
hoe, 6

M
melons, 14, 15
mushrooms, 20, 21

P
potatoes, 6
potions, 20, 21
pumpkins, 14, 15

S
saplings, 8, 10, 11, 12
seeds, 4, 6, 8, 14, 16
soil, 4, 6, 7, 10, 14
sugar cane, 14

T
trees, 8, 9, 10, 11, 12

W
water, 4, 6, 7, 14
wheat, 6, 8

Websites

Due to the changing nature of Internet links, PowerKids Press has developed
an online list of websites related to the subject of this book. This site is
updated regularly. Please use this link to access the list:
www.powerkidslinks.com/stemmc/plants